METUSELA F. ALBERT

THE
144,000
in the Book of
REVELATION.
(IT IS A LITERAL NUMBER).

To order additional copies of this book, contact:
Xlibris
844-714-8691
www.Xlibris.com
Orders@Xlibris.com

ISBN: Softcover   979-8-3694-2657-9
        EBook   979-8-3694-2658-6

Print information available on the last page

Rev. date: 07/25/2024

Contents

INTRODUCTION V

CHAPTER 1   READ - REVELATION CHAPTER 7:1-17 (KING JAMES
             VERSION). 1

CHAPTER 2   THE GREAT TRIBULATION TIME - (REVELATION 13)........... 6

CHAPTER 3   REVELATION 14:1-6 11

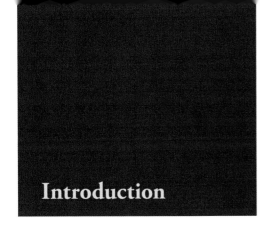

Introduction

Amongst Christianity, there are different views about the 144,000 in the Book of Revelation.

1 - Some people believe that the 144,000 refers to a "Special Group" from their <u>own Church</u> (Denomination). In other words, if you are not a member of their Church, hence you are <u>not</u> going to be part of the 144,000.

2 - Some people believe that the 144,000 are the <u>only people</u> to be saved and taken to heaven at the time of JESUS CHRIST'S return.

3 - Some people believe that the 144,000 are vegetarians / vegan.

4 - Some people believe that the keeping of the Sabbath Commandment is part of the sealing of the 144,000. According to them, if you don't keep the seventh-day Sabbath, you will <u>not</u> be sealed as part of the 144,000. Their emphasis is on the <u>seventh-day Sabbath</u> keeping, in order to be sealed. They advocate that the Sabbath is GOD'S seal. They teach that the 144,000 is <u>a symbolic</u> number.

NOTE: None of the four different views mentioned above are correct. Therefore, we need to know the truth.

WHAT DOES YOUR CHURCH TEACH ABOUT THE 144,000?

If your church teaches one of those four theories mentioned above, then know it from today that it is false.

Find out what your Church teaches on this important subject so that you are <u>not</u> caught in the confusion. Avoid being deceived by others. Don't be ignorant since the Bible is clear about *the sealing* of the 144,000 in Revelation Chapter 7.

Because of the different views in regard to this important subject, therefore, this Book you are holding is written to give you the real truth that was never being taught by the Mainline Protestant Denominations.

Actually, this subject must be understood in the <u>CONTEXT </u>OF THE TIME OF TROUBLE IN REVELATION CHAPTER 13, AND THE SEALING OF GOD'S PEOPLE, <u>just prior</u> to JESUS CHRIST'S return.

NOTE: The thirteen (13) Chapters of this Book were prepared in a <u>Chronological Order</u> to help you as understand the End Time Prophecies relating to the Second Coming of JESUS, and the transfer of His people to heaven.

Remember, <u>not</u> everyone who professes to believe in JESUS and His Commandments will be taken to heaven – (Read Matthew 7:21-24).

Stay tuned, have an open mind, and keep searching for the truth.

CHAPTER 1

READ - REVELATION CHAPTER 7:1-17 (KING JAMES VERSION).

¹ And after these things I saw four angels standing on the four corners of the earth, holding the four winds of the earth, that the wind should not blow on the earth, nor on the sea, nor on any tree.

² And I saw another angel ascending from the east, <u>having the seal of the living God</u>: and he cried with a loud voice to the four angels, to whom it was given to hurt the earth and the sea,

³ Saying, Hurt not the earth, neither the sea, nor the trees, till we have sealed the servants of our God in their foreheads.

⁴ And <u>I heard the number of them which were sealed</u>: and <u>there were sealed an hundred and forty and four thousand</u> of all the tribes of the children of Israel.

⁵ Of the tribe of Juda were sealed twelve thousand. Of the tribe of Reuben were sealed twelve thousand. Of the tribe of Gad were sealed twelve thousand.

⁶ Of the tribe of Aser were sealed twelve thousand. Of the tribe of Nephthalim were sealed twelve thousand. Of the tribe of Manasses were sealed twelve thousand.

⁷ Of the tribe of Simeon were sealed twelve thousand. Of the tribe of Levi were sealed twelve thousand. Of the tribe of Issachar were sealed twelve thousand.

⁸ Of the tribe of Zabulon were sealed twelve thousand. Of the tribe of Joseph were sealed twelve thousand. Of the tribe of Benjamin were sealed twelve thousand.

⁹ After this I beheld, and, lo, a great multitude, which no man could number, of all nations, and kindreds, and people, and tongues, stood before the throne, and before the Lamb, clothed with white robes, and palms in their hands;

¹⁰ And cried with a loud voice, saying, Salvation to our God which sitteth upon the throne, and unto the Lamb.

¹¹ And all the angels stood round about the throne, and about the elders and the four beasts, and fell before the throne on their faces, and worshipped God,

¹² Saying, Amen: Blessing, and glory, and wisdom, and thanksgiving, and honour, and power, and might, be unto our God for ever and ever. Amen.

¹³ <u>And one of the elders answered, saying unto me, What are these which are arrayed in white robes? and whence came they?</u>

¹⁴ <u>And I said unto him, Sir, thou knowest. And he said to me, These are they which came out of great tribulation, and have washed their robes, and made them white in the blood of the Lam</u>

¹⁵ Therefore are they before the throne of God, and <u>serve him</u> day and night in <u>his temple</u>: and <u>he that sitteth on the throne shall dwell among them.</u>

¹⁶ They shall hunger no more, neither thirst any more; neither shall the sun light on them, nor any heat.

¹⁷ For the Lamb which is in the midst of the throne shall feed them, and shall lead them unto living fountains of waters: and <u>God shall wipe away all tears from their eyes.</u>

....

- **DID YOU NOTICE THE <u>KEY TEXT</u> FOR THE 144,000???**

- **THE KEY TEXT IS IN REVELATION 7:14.**

<u>**And I said unto him, Sir, thou knowest. And he said to me, "These are they which came out of great tribulation, and have washed their robes, and made them white in the blood of the Lamb."**</u>

....

A <u>PICTURE</u> is worth more than a thousand words.

Please Check the timeline PICTURE (Power-Point Slide), attached below. It shows the 144,000 in the CONTEXT relating to <u>the events of the End Time Prophecies and the Second Coming of JESUS</u>. In less than five minutes, you can easily grasp the subject of the 144,000 in that <u>one picture (Power Point Slide)</u> shown below.

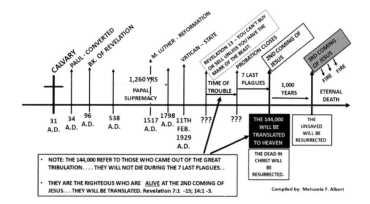

....

WHO ARE THE 144,000?

- **REVELATION 7:14 SAYS,**

And I said unto him, Sir, thou knowest. And he said to me, <u>these are they which came out of great tribulation</u>, and have washed their robes and made them white in the blood of the lamb.

AN IMPORTANT POINT TO TAKE NOTE:

The 144,000 will <u>not</u> experience death. They are the righteous who are <u>alive</u> during the time of the Second Coming of JESUS. They are <u>not</u> members of one particular denomination. Of course, nobody needs to belong to a certain denomination to be saved. Salvation is not in a denomination but in JESUS, the JEHOVAH who created heaven and earth. During the seven last plagues, none of those who are sealed will die. Death will not touch the 144,000.

THE MAIN POINT IS:
THE 144,000 CAME OUT
OF THE GREAT TRIBULATION.
Revelation 7:13-14

THE 144,000 IS A <u>LITERAL</u> NUMBER.

God said - 12,000 people from each tribe = 144,000 <u>in number</u>. God knew already who these people are. He is all knowing. He already knew who will overcome persecution during the Great Tribulation time.

Remember? At the time of Noah, eight (8) people got saved in the Ark. That was a <u>LITERAL</u> number. Before God called Noah to build the Ark, He already knew that only eight (8) people will enter the Ark before the flood.

Similarly, at the time of Sodom and Gomorrah's destruction, He knew less than 10 righteous people can be found in that city. In fact, only three (3) people escaped the destruction of Sodom and Gomorrah. Who were they? Only Lot, the nephew of Abraham and his two daughters. That was a <u>LITERAL</u> number, <u>not</u> a symbolic number.

WHAT ABOUT THE GREAT MULTITUDE AT THE TIME OF JESUS CHRIST'S RETURN?

Who are they????

The Great Multitude at the time of JESUS CHRIST'S Second Coming refers to <u>the righteous who were already dead</u>. They will be <u>resurrected</u> and taken to heaven.

....

NOTE THE DIFFERENCE: THE RESURRECTION OF THE RIGHTEOUS DEAD AT THE TIME OF JESUS' SECOND COMING IS DIFFERENT FROM THE ONES JESUS RESURRECTED AND <u>TOOK WHEN HE ASCENDED</u> TO HEAVEN IN 31 A.D.

We know that when JESUS ascended to heaven after His resurrection, He resurrected some people and took with Him to heaven. We were not told of their names.

Is it possible that the repentant thief on the Cross was taken in that group? . . . Is it possible that Abel, the brother of Cain was resurrected and taken also? . . . Is it possible that Lazarus, the brother of Mary and Martha, was resurrected and taken by JESUS?

Remember, Moses was <u>already resurrected</u> and taken to heaven before the children of Israel entered the Promised land, Canaan.

<u>THE RESURRECTION OF THE GREAT MULTITUDE</u>.

The resurrection of <u>the righteous dead</u> when JESUS returns the second time, <u>is the resurrection of the Great Multitude. This is a different group from the 144,000 people.</u>

CHAPTER 2

THE GREAT TRIBULATION TIME

This Prophecy of the Great Tribulation Time is mentioned in Revelation Chapter 13.

A time is coming where you <u>cannot</u> buy or sell, unless you have <u>the Mark of the Beast</u> and <u>the Number of the Beast's Name, which is 666</u>. Only when this prophecy in Revelation 13 starts to happen, then we can be certain that JESUS is <u>SOON</u> to return.

At the meantime, while we are waiting for the return of JESUS, we need to be ready before <u>death</u> strikes. But don't be disheartened when death hits. Why? Because Death is only a temporary separation from our loved ones. If we were dead, then the next event for the dead is the Resurrection, either at the <u>second</u> OR the <u>third</u> return of JESUS. (Check the diagram to understand the difference between the Resurrection at the <u>second</u> and <u>third</u> return of JESUS).

The Resurrection of the dead at the <u>second</u> coming of JESUS is called = the <u>First</u> Resurrection. This is the Resurrection of the <u>Righteous</u>. This Resurrection takes place <u>at the beginning</u> of the 1,000 years.

And the Resurrection of the dead at the <u>third</u> coming of JESUS is called = the <u>Second</u> Resurrection. This is the Resurrection of the <u>Wicked</u>. This Resurrection takes place at the end of the 1,000 years.

It is at the third Coming of JESUS that He comes back with the Holy City – the New Jerusalem to establish on earth.

At the same time, Fire comes down to destroy the wicked. The wicked will die eternally. This is called second death which is the wages of sin. (Romans 6:23).

NOTE: The second death will take place at the end of the Millennium (1,000 years).

In the New Earth, there will be no more sin, no more pain, no more death, no more crying, no more suffering. JESUS will be our GOD, dwelling in the city.

....

Actually, the delay of Jesus Christ's second coming should not worry us as believers, if we are in Christ at the point of death. Death is only a temporary sleep and the resurrection is the assurance for those died in the LORD.

....

NOTE: When Preachers / Pastors / Evangelists / Bishops, etc., speak of the signs of JESUS' soon return, but if the Prophecy mentioned in Revelation Chapter 13 has not started yet, don't get carried away by them.

Don't expect JESUS to return soon since the Prophecy in Revelation 13 must take place first.

POINT: THOSE WHO ARE ALIVE WHEN THE PROPHECY IN REVELATION 13 BEGINS, THEY SHOULD KNOW FOR SURE THAT THE RETURN OF JESUS IS VERY SOON BECAUSE THAT IS THE CLEAREST SIGN THAT WILL CAUSE THE GREAT TRIBULATION TO HAPPEN.

While we are waiting for the return of JESUS, we need to be sure of the clearest sign about His soon return.

The disciples believed that JESUS was going to return in their time. And many great preachers advocated the soon return of JESUS in the past, yet we are still here. It is now, July 2024, but JESUS has not returned yet.

<u>After the Great Tribulation time, the Close of Probation will happen</u>, and to be followed by the 7 last plagues (Revelation 16), then the return of JESUS will take place, as Prophesied. (Study the Chart provided).

. . . .

Many of GOD'S righteous people <u>will die</u> during <u>the Great Tribulation time (Revelation 13)</u>. But that is only the <u>first</u> death (a temporary sleep), <u>not</u> eternal death. They will make up part of the group called – <u>THE GREAT MULTITUDE</u>, which is different from the 144,000.

Those who died in the LORD during the Great Tribulation Time will make <u>up part</u> of the group (The Great Multitude) that will be resurrected at JESUS CHRIST'S <u>second coming</u>, then be taken to heaven.

But, <u>the 144,000 is a different group</u>.

»»

A VERY IMPORTANT POINT TO TAKE NOTE.

THE GREAT TRIBULATION TIME MENTIONED IN REVELATION CHAPTER 13 IS THE <u>BIG EVENT</u> THAT MUST HAPPEN <u>FIRST</u> BEFORE THE OTHER EVENTS SUCH AS THE CLOSE OF PROBATION AND THE SEVEN LAST PLAGUES. THEN THE SECOND COMING OF JESUS.

. . . .

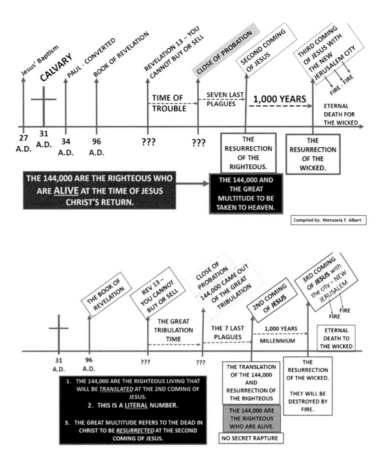

Thank you for purchasing this Book to enrich your understanding about the 144,000 in Revelation Chapter 7.

....

THE SEQUENCE OF EVENTS LEADING TO THE RETURN OF JESUS.

– The Great Tribulation Time - (Revelation 13).

– The 144,000 will be victorious - (Revelation 14).

– The Close of Probation - (Revelation 15).

– The Seven Last Plagues - (Revelation 16).

– The Second Coming of JESUS <u>After</u> the Seven Last Plagues.

– The 144,000 will be <u>Translated</u> like Enoch.

– The <u>dead in Christ</u> will be <u>resurrected</u> (THE GREAT MULTITUDE)– (Rev 20:4-6).

– The 144,000 love GOD and keep His COMMANDMENTS.

– The 144,000 will be <u>sealed</u> <u>before</u> the Seven Last Plagues.

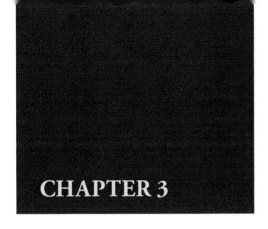

CHAPTER 3

REVELATION 14:1-6

1. And I looked and lo, a Lamb stood on Mount Zion, and with Him <u>a hundred forty and four thousand, having His Father's name written in their foreheads.</u>

² And I heard a voice from Heaven as the voice of many waters, and as the voice of a great thunder, and I heard the voice of harpers harping with their harps.

³ And they sang, as it were, a new song before the throne, and before the four living beings and the elders; and no man could learn that song, <u>except the hundred and forty and four thousand who were redeemed from the earth.</u>

⁴ <u>These are they that were not defiled with women, for they are virgins.</u> These are they that follow the Lamb whithersoever He goeth. <u>These were redeemed from among men,</u> being the firstfruits unto God and to the Lamb.

⁵ <u>And in their mouth was found no guile, for they are without fault before the throne of God.</u>

⁶ And I saw another angel fly in the midst of heaven, having the everlasting Gospel to preach unto them that dwell on the earth, and to every nation and kindred, and tongue and people.

....

POINT: The 144,000 are men who are <u>virgins like Joseph</u> before he married Mary.

FURTHER INFORMATION

– GOD'S <u>seal</u> upon the righteous is <u>not</u> the Sabbath.

– There is <u>NO</u> secret Rapture – (Revelation 1:7).

– JESUS is the <u>only GOD</u> who sits on the THRONE – (Revelation 4:1-11; 21:5-7).

If you did <u>not</u> know yet that JESUS was the GOD (JEHOVAH) of Abraham who created heaven and earth before his incarnation into human flesh through Mary at Bethlehem, then check this link –

www.Jesus-theGodofAbraham.com

In other words, if you still believe in a Trinity GOD theory, then click the link above and read the Books written to help your understanding about JESUS.

PUBLISHED ON MARCH 04, 2011

PUBLISHED ON JUNE 01, 2021

THERE IS NO TRINITY GOD IN HEAVEN.

BOOK - PUBLISHED ON
DECEMBER 16, 2020

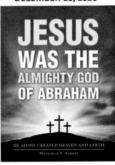

BOOK - PUBLISHED ON
JANUARY 22, 2021

BOOK - PUBLISHED ON
SEPTEMBER 12, 2021

PUBLISHED ON AUGUST 17, 2021.

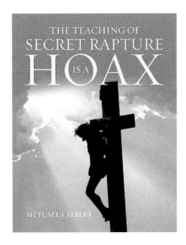

BOOK # 8

PUBLISHED
ON MARCH
21, 2023.

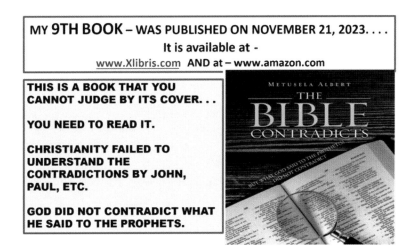

MY 9TH BOOK – WAS PUBLISHED ON NOVEMBER 21, 2023. . . .
It is available at -
www.Xlibris.com AND at – www.amazon.com

THIS IS A BOOK THAT YOU
CANNOT JUDGE BY ITS COVER. . .

YOU NEED TO READ IT.

CHRISTIANITY FAILED TO
UNDERSTAND THE
CONTRADICTIONS BY JOHN,
PAUL, ETC.

GOD DID NOT CONTRADICT WHAT
HE SAID TO THE PROPHETS.

Again, thank you for your interest in learning the truth about JESUS, our only GOD in heaven who became human flesh by <u>the incarnation process</u> to die at Calvary as our Sin Bearer / Savior.

Should JESUS CHRIST return at your time while you are still <u>alive, you can be part of the 144,000.</u>

<u>When a NATIONAL LAW is enforced by the government that you cannot buy or sell, unless you have the Beast and the mumber of his name which is 666 (Revelation 13),</u> try and be part of the 144,000. HOW?

1. Choose to stand up for the truth by GOD'S help.

2. Make JESUS CHRIST your <u>only GOD</u> and reject the BEAST and his number 666.

3. Reject the belief that says, three persons making up one GOD in heaven.

4. Reject the Trinity GOD theory.

5. Reject the Triune GOD theory.

6. Reject the Duality GOD theory.

7. Reject the belief that says, GOD the Father, GOD the Son, and GOD the Holy Spirit, make one GOD.

8. Reject the belief that says, GOD created baby sinners from Adam.

9. Reject the belief that says, Sin is by nature.

10. Reject the belief that says, the death of JESUS already saved everyone at Calvary.

11. Reject the belief that says, our past, present, and future sins, were all forgiven at Calvary. Forgiven before we were born.

12. Reject the belief that says, Jesus was born by GOD the Father in heaven before the angels were created.

13. Reject the belief that says, the Holy Spirit is a third person in heaven.

14. Reject the belief that says, JESUS is the Holy Spirit.

Thank you for purchasing this Book to find out the truth about the 144,000 and relevant topics briefly explained.

GOD bless.

Printed in the United States
by Baker & Taylor Publisher Services